# Take care! POISONOUS AUSTRALIAN ANIMALS

## STRUAN SUTHERLAND

M.D., D.SC., F.R.C.P.A., F.R.A.C.P.

 HYLAND HOUSE

By the same author:

*Family Guide to Dangerous Animals and Plants of Australia*
*Venomous Creatures of Australia*
*Australian Animal Toxins: The creatures, their toxins and care of the poisoned patient.*
*Hydroponics for Everyone*

## ACKNOWLEDGEMENTS

Thanks are due to Miss Anne Godden and Miss Angela Ridsdale for advice and expert editing of this book. Mrs Mary Galea and Mrs Marjory Davey kindly typed the manuscript. Thanks, too, to Leonie Stott for help with the cartoons.
Some photographs were kindly provided by Dr Covacevich and Messrs Gillet, Tannner and Worrell. I should like to thank Telecom, too, for allowing the use of their diagrams on resuscitation.

First published in 1992 by
Hyland House Publishing Pty Limited
10 Hyland Street
South Yarra
Victoria 3141
An earlier and smaller edition of this book was first published in 1983.

© Struan K. Sutherland 1991

National Library of Australia
cataloguing-in-publication data:

Sutherland, Struan K. (Struan Keith), 1936–
   Take care!: poisonous Australian animals.

   2nd ed.
   ISBN 0 947062 87 4.
   ISBN 1 875657 01 0 (pbk.)

   1. Poisonous animals – Australia – Juvenile literature. I. Title.
591.690994

Designed and illustrated by Leonie Stott
Typeset by Butler Graphics Pty Limited, Hawthorn, Victoria
Printed and bound by Dai Nippon Printing Company Limited, Hong Kong

# Contents

# Contents cont.

# Introduction

Holidays in the country or by the sea are great fun – much better than being at school. Who wants to have a fabulous holiday messed up by an angry snake or ruined by jellyfish stings? No one! The purpose of this book is to say something about our most important poisonous creatures – some of which are the most dangerous in the world – and explain how not to be hurt by them. None of them is particularly keen to bite or sting people, but sadly this often happens, and so the modern types of first aid are explained.

No one goes off camping for a few days without the right clothes, good equipment and plenty of tucker. All campers should spare a few moments to learn how to avoid poisonous bites and stings. They can then settle down to enjoy the wonders of nature in the countryside rather than end up reading about them in a hospital bed.

## DEDICATION

To all children who have died of snake bites – especially Maree V. aged 3 years.

# Why some animals have a poisonous bite or sting

All animals need food and the venomous ones like fresh food. They use their poison to kill their prey quickly with as little trouble as possible. Why get into a fight when you can win with a secret weapon?

Snakes and spiders have two hollow teeth (*fangs*) which can put poison (*venom*) into the creatures they bite. The venom is made in two *sacs* like very small plastic bags and it is squeezed out as the fangs go into the victim, often an insect or mouse. The venom kills the victim quickly so that the snake or spider can eat its dinner in peace and quiet.

Some animals, like jellyfish, have millions of tiny stinging spikes which are fired into prawns or fish. They die in seconds.

If people are poisoned by dangerous snakes or spiders the venom may slowly damage the nerves of their bodies so that they may become weaker and weaker. They may even die some hours later if they are not treated by a doctor.

The good news is that all hospitals have special medicines (antivenoms) which can quickly stop the venom working. Before antivenoms were made many children and adults died from bites and stings. Nowadays they almost always get better and go home next day with rather an exciting story to tell their mates!

## *SPECIAL NOTE FOR PARENTS!*

Never let children collect snakes. If young children say they have had contact with a snake, please believe them. Remember that a young child may sometimes describe the snake as a stick or a rope.

# How to avoid bites and stings

## SNAKE BITE

- Leave snakes alone.
- Wear shoes, socks and jeans in 'snake country'. Do not wear sandals or thongs.
- Never put your hands into hollow logs or thick grass without looking first.
- Turn your shoes upside down and shake them before putting them on.
- When in the bush check your sleeping bag, towel, clothes, etc. before using them.
- Always use a torch around camps and farm-houses at night. Remember most snakes are active on summer nights.
- Make sure barns and sheds are kept free of mice and rats which may attract snakes, and help keep the grass well cut, particularly in playgrounds and other places you go to.

## SPIDER BITE

Don't touch spiders! 99.9 per cent of them have fangs and can poison you, even though most are not likely to make you sick. Take special care in places like the backs of sheds or outside toilets or when playing near old rubbish, wood heaps, etc.

## DANGEROUS SEA CREATURES

Don't swim in the sea by yourself and never go into the sea in the tropics when Box jellyfish are about. Always wear sandshoes if exploring tropical reefs. Never pick up octopuses or any other sea creatures without asking if they are poisonous. Wear gloves when touching fish.

# First aid

## SNAKE BITE

Even though some snakes are not dangerous it is best to treat all snake bites as if they were dangerous and give the victim first aid. A snake usually bites near the ankle or the hand and so it is easy to use first aid. Remember, never make cuts over the snake bite or put a tight bandage around the top of the leg or arm, but use the correct method of first aid described below. Don't wash the bitten area because hospitals do a special test on the fang marks. This lets the doctor know what type of snake has made the bite.

### First aid for snake bite: the 'Pressure/ immobilisation method'

Look at the pictures on pages 9 and 10.

1 Put a broad firm bandage around the limb and on the bitten area. Crepe bandages are best but any flexible material will do, e.g. tear up clothing or old towels into strips. Pantyhose is also suitable.

2 The bandage should be as tight as you would bind a sprained ankle.

3 Bandage as much of the limb as possible.

4 Keep the limb as still as possible. Bind some type of splint to the limb, e.g. a piece of timber, spade, or anything which doesn't bend.

5 Take the victim to a doctor or hospital *as quickly as possible*. Try to bring a car *as close as possible* to the victim. If that's impossible see if you can make a stretcher and carry him or her to the car. Remember the limb should be kept still so if the bite is on a leg the victim shouldn't walk.

6   Leave the bandages and splint on until medical care is reached.
It's a good idea to practise this kind of first aid sometimes,
especially if you live in the country or will be going into the bush
for a holiday.

# PRESSURE/IMMOBILISATION METHOD OF FIRST AID

## For bites to the forearm

**1** Put a broad firm bandage round the bitten area up to the elbow, as described in nos. 1 and 2 opposite. Bandage as much of the fingers as possible. Make sure the victim can still bend the elbow.

**2** Put a splint under the arm and bind it to the arm.

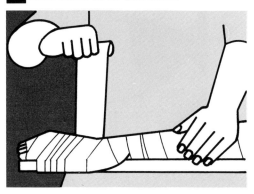

**3** Put the arm in a sling.

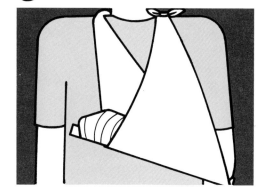

# For bites on the leg

**1** Put a broad firm bandage round the bitten area. Don't take off any clothes like jeans but cut the seams if they can't be pushed out of the way, and keep the leg as still as possible while you are bandaging.

**2** Make the bandage as tight as for a sprained ankle.

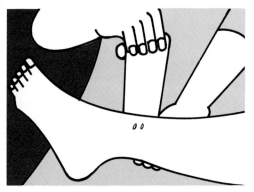
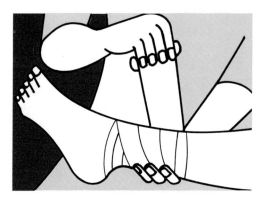

**3** Bandage as much of the leg as possible, especially the toes.

**4** Put a splint beside the bandage and bind that to the leg to help keep the leg still.

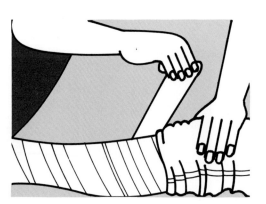
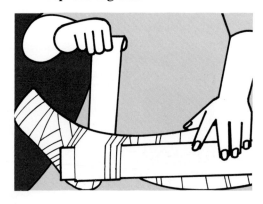

The bandages and splint should be quite comfortable so that they can be left on for several hours. They should not be taken off until the victim has reached a doctor or hospital. The doctor will decide when to remove the bandages.

> ## REMEMBER!
> First aid is only *first* aid.
> The victim should go to a doctor or hospital as soon as possible.

## SPIDER BITE

The Pressure-immobilisation method of first aid is used also for Funnel-web spider bites. Red-back spider bites don't need any special first aid because the venom works very slowly. Just take the victim (and spider in a jar) to hospital as soon as possible. If the Red-back spider bite is painful, put a plastic bag filled with a little ice and water on the painful area.

No special first aid is required for bites by other spiders, such as the White-tailed spider, the Black House or Window spider and Huntsman spiders. Usually very little effect is produced by their bites. If the bite is painful, put a plastic bag filled with a little ice and water over the painful area.

## AUSTRALIAN PARALYSIS TICK BITE

The tick should be carefully removed as soon as possible (see page 43). If the victim is feeling ill and the bite is on the arm or leg, use the Pressure/immobilisation method of first aid, if possible, to slow the movement of any poison which has been squeezed out of the tick during its removal.

## BEE STINGS

Scrape the sting and venom sac off the stung area and put a plastic bag filled with a little ice and water on the stung area.

## EUROPEAN AND ENGLISH WASPS, AND JUMPER AND BULL ANTS

Put a plastic bag filled with a little ice and water over the stung area.

# HEART-LUNG RESUSCITATION IN BASIC LIFE SUPPORT

**1** Place the victim flat on his back on a hard surface. If unconscious, open airway – lift up neck, push forehead back, clear out mouth if necessary, observe for breathing.

**2** If not breathing, begin artificial breathing – 3 quick breaths by mouth to mouth, holding the nose closed.

**3** Check pulse in neck. If pulse is absent, begin artificial circulation – depress lower end of breast bone (sternum), 4cm to 5cm, less for small children.

**4** One rescuer – 15 compressions, rate 60 to 80 per minute, 2 quick breaths. Two rescuers – 5 compressions, rate 60 to 80 per minute, 1 breath in 5 seconds.
Continue uninterrupted until trained assistance is available.
The compression rate is 60 to 80 per minute whether there is one operator or two.

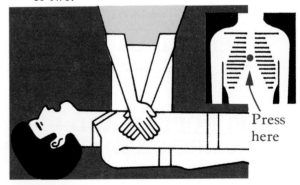

Press here

## SEVERE REACTIONS TO BEE, EUROPEAN AND ENGLISH WASP AND JUMPER AND BULL ANT STINGS

If you know that the person who has been stung is sensitive to these stings and will suffer a severe reaction, apply the Pressure/immobilisation method of first aid to the stung area. Assist the victim's breathing if necessary (see opposite) and take the victim to a doctor or hospital as soon as possible.

## PLATYPUS STING

Do not apply the Pressure/immobilisation method of first aid. Iced water may give some relief from pain, but most patients need an injection of painkillers by a doctor.

## SEA ANIMALS: BLUE-RINGED OCTOPUS AND CONUS SHELLS

Use the Pressure/immobilisation method. Mouth to mouth resuscitation or some other type of help with breathing may be needed also. The pictures on the opposite page tell you how to do this.

## BOX JELLY FISH OR 'SEA WASP'

As soon as possible pour kitchen vinegar over the tentacles to kill them. Never use methylated spirits or alcohol.

## BLUE BOTTLE OR PORTUGUESE MAN-OF-WAR

Stings from this creature are treated by washing any tentacles off with water and then putting a plastic bag filled with a little ice and water over the stung area. Tests have shown that water is better than vinegar.

## STINGRAYS

Put a plastic bag filled with a little ice and water over the stung area. If bleeding occurs, apply firm pressure over the area. All stingray stings should be seen by a doctor.

## STONEFISH AND OTHER STINGING FISH

Try bathing the sting in warm water. Antivenom and special drugs will be needed for bad Stonefish stings. Stings from fish are very painful, but usually the pain does not last long.

*Tasmanian Tiger snake sunning itself.*

# Snakes

Snakes are reptiles. They are cold blooded animals and are usually more active after they have been warmed up by the sun. They shed their skin regularly and go into hiding while this is happening. Since a snake has no eyelids it gives a steady, unblinking look which frightens many people. Its eyesight and sense of smell is quite good but it is completely deaf. It picks up vibrations from the ground through its body so it's a good idea, if snakes are about, for you to stomp along (in boots) as loudly as possible. If the snake feels you are coming it will slither away long before you get there. Some snakes lay eggs and others produce their babies alive.

Some funny stories are told about snakes which are not true. Snakes don't swallow their young to protect them. If they eat another snake it's for their dinner! Snakes will die any time, not just at sunset. A saucer of milk will not attract a snake, nor will music. Snakes are just snakes and are not magical except in some stories. Like most animals they only want to be left alone to live their lives in peace and usually bite people only when they are frightened.

There are more than 100 types of snakes in Australia and at least 18 are dangerous to people. Some of the most important ones are described in this book.

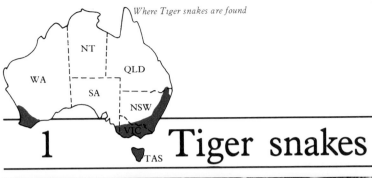

# 1 Tiger snakes

Tiger snakes usually have yellowish stripes like a tiger and when they're annoyed they can be as dangerous as a real tiger!

There are black Tiger snakes which live in the south-west of Western Australia, the Flinders Ranges in South Australia and in Tasmania and the Bass Strait Islands. They don't have yellow stripes, but they're just as dangerous so look out for them too!

Tiger snakes grow to about 1 metre in length. They don't lay eggs. Even the new born baby snakes can bite and should never be touched!

They are often found near rivers and dams and they love eating frogs. They also like mice and on hot summer evenings will hunt them round farms and outer suburban houses. They will even come into kitchens and bedrooms!

Snake bites are often caused by Tiger snakes so be very careful on summer evenings when they are out hunting.

 ***First aid for Tiger snake bites —***
• Pressure/immobilisation technique, see pages 9-10.

*Where Brown snakes are found*

# 2 Brown snakes

There are a number of types of brown snakes and they are all very dangerous. The most important is the Eastern or Common Brown snake. Its colour varies from light brown to very dark brown and it is slender and very fast moving. It may grow as long as 2.4 metres.

Brown snakes prefer dry places and often come around farms looking for mice and rats which they enjoy eating. Unlike the tiger snakes, the brown snakes lay eggs, but like them they are deadly. Their venom is the second most poisonous in Australia. When a Brown snake is angry it may wind itself up into an 'S' shape and so people are often bitten on the knee or higher.

Apart from catching rats the only good thing about this snake is that it is the only very dangerous Australian snake which *usually* goes to sleep when the sun sets. Sometimes it goes to sleep in a camper's sleeping bag! So don't forget to shake your bag out before tucking yourself up for the night.

 ***First aid for Brown snake bites —***
• Pressure/immobilisation technique, see pages 9-10.

# 3 Red-bellied Black snake

When the white settlers arrived in Eastern Australia they found the bush absolutely teeming with these snakes. The poor settlers were scared stiff and worked hard to kill off as many as they could. In fact one wealthy settler, knowing that there were no wild snakes in Ireland, actually brought out a shipload of soil to put around his house in the hope that it would keep the snakes away. This snake is far less dangerous than the other snakes described in this book.

It may grow to 2.5 metres and its red sides and tummy make it easy to see. The babies are born alive, not in eggs.

It has a fairly gentle nature and generally will only bite if it is really annoyed.

It loves swimming and is very fond of eating other snakes, even other Red-bellied Black snakes. It is not very often seen in zoos as it tends quietly to eat up all the other snakes when no one is watching!

*First aid for Red-bellied Black snake bites —*
• Pressure/immobilisation technique, see pages 9-10.

*Where Death Adders are found*

# 4 Death Adder

This is a very dangerous snake which looks quite different from other Australian snakes. Its body can be 1 metre long, is thick and ends in a funny little spiky tail. This snake does not lay eggs.

The worst thing about this snake is that it likes to come out at night and lie half buried in leaves on bush tracks. It wiggles its little tail and then kills any mouse or rat which wanders up to see what's going on. Other snakes usually move away if they know a human is walking towards them, but not the Death Adder! It stays perfectly still and bites very quickly if it is touched.

Its fangs are long and the venom is very strong. Some people call these snakes 'Deaf Adders' since they don't get out of the way when someone walks towards them. However, like all snakes, they do not have proper ears but pick up vibrations from the ground made as the human tramps along.

Use a torch at night and you are much less likely to be bitten by a Death Adder.

 **First aid for Death Adder bites —**
• Pressure/immobilisation technique, see pages 9-10.

THE DEATH ADDER ADDS UP HIS DAY'S KILL!

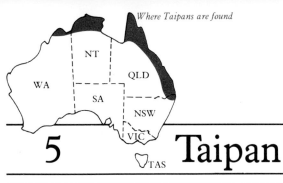

# 5 Taipan

This is the longest highly venomous snake in Australia and may reach 3.35 metres in length. The young hatch out of eggs. It is very shy and people often don't know that they have been near one. This is just as well because, if cornered, it can be most vicious. Often the Taipan bites again and again — so quickly that it is just a blur. Its fangs are the longest of any Australian snake (the record is 13 millimetres).

Until an antivenom was made, most people bitten by Taipans died because of the strength and amount of venom it injects. Several years ago a little boy of four was attacked by a Taipan and died a few minutes later. It is most unusual for people to die so quickly but he had a great many bites.

Taipans often hunt near farm buildings or on garbage tips. They feed on rats and mice and will sometimes catch birds. When they are 'milked' of their venom in the laboratory the average amount of venom taken is enough to kill 12,000 guinea pigs! Thank heavens Taipans are usually frightened by people and race off in the opposite direction!

 *First aid for Taipan bites —*
• Pressure/immobilisation technique, see pages 9-10.

*Where Mulga snakes are found*

# 6 Mulga snake

This is Australia's heaviest dangerous snake. It is sometimes called the 'King Brown snake', although it is not related to the Brown snakes described in this book. It grows to over 3 metres in length and produces more venom than any other Australian snake. Although the venom is not quite as strong as that of the other common poisonous snakes, a bite by this snake may be very serious. It often makes a few big bruises around the bites as its big heavy head strikes against the person. The bites are usually painful with a lot of swelling.

The Mulga snake eats many rats, mice, lizards and birds as well as other snakes. Rabbit burrows make a fine home for the snake and its eggs. Mulga snakes taste good and are a favourite food of Aborigines and bushmen, although shopping for that particular dinner has often proved more dangerous than a visit to the supermarket!

*First aid for Mulga snake bites —*
• Pressure/immobilisation technique, see pages 9-10.

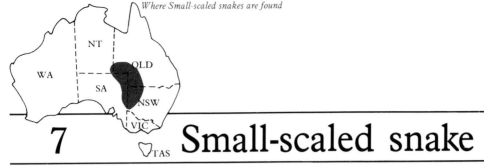

# 7 Small-scaled snake

This snake, which is also called the Fierce snake, has caused a lot of excitement lately amongst scientists. When it was found alive in Western Queensland in 1976, it was the first time it had been seen for about 100 years. Since then, many more have been found and the venom has been tested in the laboratory for the first time. To everyone's surprise, the Small-scaled snake has the most poisonous snake venom in the world. Fortunately, there have been very few records of people being bitten by this snake, but now that it is being kept in zoos and collections, bites may be more common!

The Small-scaled snake is closely related to the Taipan and some people call it the 'Western Taipan'. Its colour is darker than the Taipan and the longest one found so far measured 1.93 metres. Like the Taipan it lays eggs, but is far better tempered and would probably have to be hit with a stick before it became a 'fierce snake'! Usually it lives in deep cracks in the ground where it feeds on rats. The amount of venom it can produce is enough to kill 250,000 mice — so it's best left alone!

 *First aid for Small-scaled snake bites* —
• Pressure/immobilisation technique, see pages 9-10.

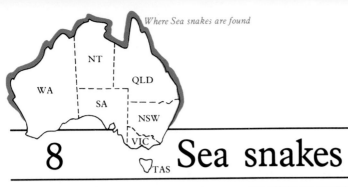

# 8 Sea snakes

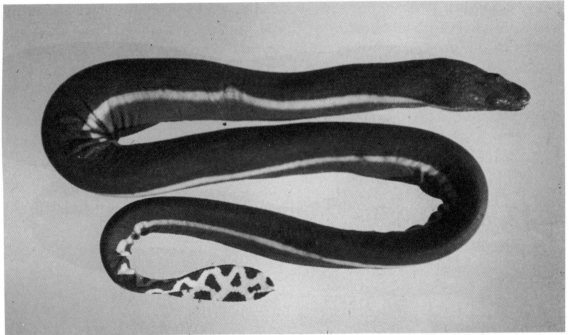

At least 26 types of sea snake swim about in the tropical waters of Australia. Sometimes one will be found down south. Many are quite poisonous but they don't often bite people. The first aid for a sea snake bite is the same as for land snakes. The doctor may have to give the victim sea snake antivenom. If this is not handy, then Tiger snake antivenom can be used.

Sea snakes are easily identified because they have a paddle-shaped tail. Most spend all their lives at sea. Sometimes they meet together in huge crowds called *slicks* drifting along on the surface of the sea. They can take a huge breath and then dive quickly deep under the sea to catch fish or prawns. They have a big lung that goes almost the length of their bodies and this can hold enough air for some snakes to dive as deep as 100 metres and stay under the water for several hours.

The babies of sea snakes are born at sea, although one type wriggles ashore and lays eggs. Sea snakes shed their skin at least once a month so that their skin is always free from any slime which would slow them down.

Prawn fishermen know to watch out for sea snakes, especially if they catch a group of them in a net at night. The crew quickly run to the other end of the boat — and I don't blame them!

Sometimes eels are mistaken for sea snakes and give people a fright. Eels are easy to recognise. They have no nostrils or scales, but they do have gills and fins as well as a good set of sharp (non poisonous) teeth. They are fish, but sea snakes are reptiles like the land snakes.

*First aid for Sea snake bites —*
• Pressure/immobilisation technique, see pages 9-10.

THAT THIN LOG IN THE SEA MIGHT SUDDENLY COME TO LIFE!

*Where Red-back spiders are found*

# 9 Red-back spider

(female pictured)

Although it seems a good joke when this spider bites someone on the bottom while they are sitting on a toilet seat, the owner of the bottom is never amused!

Every year hundreds of Australians need Red-back spider anti-venom — and most Red-back spider bites would not happen if people only took a bit more care.

The Red-back is found in most gardens, in old sheds and other quiet dark places, as well as out in the bush. Only the female's bite

32

makes people ill and the bright red or orange stripe on her behind is one of nature's clearest warnings of danger.

Usually she hides away in a corner of her untidy web, which she builds in some dark cool place, and only pops out when some insect or beetle has got stuck to the web. When she is guarding her egg sacs (and these may contain as many as 2 000 babies), she is more likely to bite any one who disturbs the web.

Generally the Red-back only bites human skin if it is pushed close to her, as when the owner comes to put on a pair of old jeans or gloves in which she has made her home. One way people often get bitten is when the spider is picked up with rubbish.

The Red-back's tiny bite hardly hurts at first but soon becomes very painful. After some hours the bitten person may have pain in other parts of the body and be sweating heavily. The victims do not get very sick for many hours and they all get better very quickly when given antivenom.

***First aid for Red-back spider bites***
- Seek medical care.
- Do not panic! The venom works very slowly.

*Where Sydney Funnel-web spiders are found*

NT

WA

QLD

SA

NSW

VIC

TAS

# 10 Funnel-web spiders

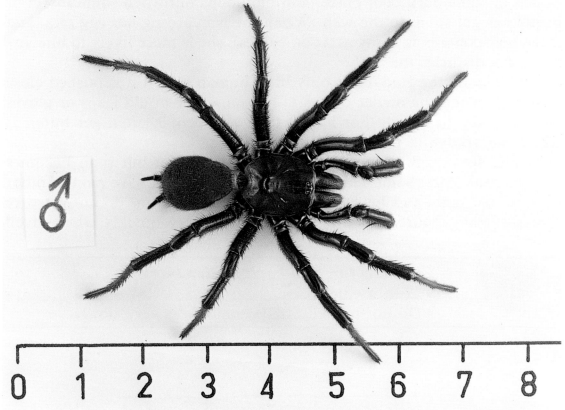

0 1 2 3 4 5 6 7 8

(male pictured)

Australia could do without these spiders! The most important one is the Sydney Funnel-web spider which is only found in an area covering 160 kilometres from the centre of Sydney. It really is the most dangerous spider in the world since its bites are known to have killed 3 children in less than 2 hours after they were bitten.

It is a very strange spider. The male Funnel-web kills people, while with other spiders the female is the most deadly. Its venom hardly makes dogs or cats sick at all, but if people are badly poisoned all their muscles may twitch, they sweat heavily, their heart beats terribly fast and then they become unconscious. Fortunately, most bitten people don't get much poison because usually it falls off the tips of the spider's big fangs just before the bite.

Funnel-web spiders like cool damp places to live in, but when the male is grown up he becomes a wanderer. He likes to roam into houses, especially if heavy rain has made the outside too wet for walking about. He is very bad tempered and stands up high with his fangs ready to bite if anyone comes near him. Great care must be taken, especially at night, so that you don't walk on him or accidentally pick him up. Turn on the light or use a torch and wear slippers or shoes. Check for spiders before you pick up clothes or put them on.

The first-aid for Funnel-web spider bite—which may save your life— is the same as for snake bite. Fortunately, an antivenom is now available in hospitals and people are no longer in such danger from this horrible spider.

***First aid for Sydney Funnel-web spider bites —***
• Pressure/immobilisation technique, see pages 9-10.

THE WORLD'S NASTIEST AND MOST DANGEROUS SPIDER

CHAMP

YAH! YAH!

SOB!

SOB!

3  1  2

# 11 White-tailed spider

This small spider is found at some time of the year in practically every house in Australia. It has a dark brown body, which is sausage shaped. Usually it has a small white spot on the tip of its tail. Being a hunting spider, it does not spin a web, but quietly prowls around looking for some sleepy insect to grab.

Quite often the White-tailed spider decides to have a rest in bedclothes or clothing that have been left on the floor. Bathroom towels are another favourite place. When the bed is made up, the White-tailed spider may find

36

itself suddenly tucked in, deep amongst the sheets, wondering how on earth to get out. Later on when a sleepy human gets into the bed and starts to squash the spider it gives a small bite. The bite is usually fairly painless. In most cases, it causes no damage but sometimes the bitten area becomes very painful some hours later. A few people develop a nasty ulcer.

It is very important always to shake bedclothes, or towels, etc. which have been left lying around for some time.

 ***First aid for White-tailed spider bites —***
• See page 11.

CHECK YOUR BED FOR A MANY LEGGED AND MULTI-EYED VISITOR

# 12 Black House or Window spider

(Photo: Vern Draffin)

This spider is found around most houses. It makes an untidy funnel-shaped web in the corner of windows and in crevices. The web itself looks a bit like lace. This spider is about as black as a spider can be, and generally hides during the day. At night it can usually be seen pottering around repairing its web or wrapping up freshly caught prey.

A bite from this spider can be very painful. Some people have felt quite sick for a few hours after the bite and they may do a great deal of vomiting.

Nobody has been known to have died from this spider's bite, but it should be treated very carefully. In particular, very large specimens are sometimes found in the bush. Be very careful when collecting firewood, and roll the logs over and inspect them closely before you pick them up.

 *First aid for Black House or Window spider bites —*
• See page 11.

DON'T POKE YOUR FINGER IN THIS VERY BLACK SPIDER'S WEB!

# 13 Huntsman spiders

(Photo: Vern Draffin)

These spiders grow to be great big fellows and are quite common in houses throughout Australia in summer. Although they give people terrible frights, it is believed that most of them are quite harmless. They do have quite big fangs, but their venom is very weak and they only bite if they are being really roughly treated.

We have put them here in this book because lots of people are scared stiff of them. They call them 'Tarantulas', which they are not. Tarantulas are not found in Australia and, believe it or not, Tarantulas are thought to be quite harmless anyway!

Huntsman spiders do a very good job crawling across walls and ceilings, wiping out mosquitoes and other annoying creatures. The good thing about spiders is that they don't damage the environment or affect the ozone layer like some insect sprays.

40

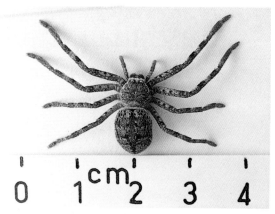

(Young Huntsman spider. Photo Vern Draffin)

I like to leave the Huntsman spiders roaming around the house until they start getting quite large. Then they can be swept out of the house with a straw broom. It is best to be wide awake when doing this, as the spiders can duck and weave like a good footballer.

Huntsman spiders occasionally can decide to hide behind the sunshade in a car. When the driver lowers the sunshade, the spider drops onto his or her lap. Lots of things can happen in the next few seconds!

 *First aid for Huntsman spider bites —*
• See page 11.

WHEN YOUR HUNTSMEN GROWS UP, IT'S TIME FOR IT TO LEAVE HOME!

# 14 Australian Paralysis tick

A family picnic in 'Tick country' may never be forgotten. Like female mosquitoes, ticks feed on the blood of animals through a little hole in their skin. They like hot meals and so feed only on warm blooded animals like people, dogs and cats. As the tiny tick quietly sucks up its dinner from your body, its saliva escapes into the skin. The saliva is poisonous and can weaken the nerves of its victim. It is the most dangerous tick in the world and at least 17 children have died from paralysis caused by its saliva in New South Wales alone since 1904.

The tick goes through three stages during its life and at each stage it must feed on blood. The last stage is the important one: the tiny nymph tick climbs to the tops of bushes hoping to be brushed onto a passing animal. Once on the animal the nymph, which is the size of a pin's head, buries its mouth parts into the skin. Over the next 3 or 4 days it fills itself with blood and may become as large as a child's finger nail. Then it usually falls off and lays its eggs but it may stay on the skin and, after a time, it will cause paralysis. The longer it stays the more poisonous its saliva becomes.

Only the female tick feeds on animals, the male actually makes a hole on the female's back and drinks her blood. She doesn't seem to mind and even lets him mate at the same time!

After you have been in 'Tick country' you should look for ticks on your body over the next few days. Get someone else to look into the places you can't see like the top of your head or your ears.

Ticks should be removed by carefully levering them out. Curved scissors make a good tool and should be carried in the first aid kit if you are going to camp in bush where there are ticks. A doctor should be seen if the victim feels tired or weak. People sometimes lose their appetites or they can't read easily or their muscles may feel stiff and clumsy if they are getting tick paralysis. Sometimes you never find the tick and you still fall ill. An antitoxin has been made and all patients who are treated in time now get better.

Look for ticks on your dog, too, especially in places like the ears. If he loses his appetite and looks ill or becomes clumsy when he is getting up and walking, take him to the vet and tell the vet he has been in 'Tick country'.

*First aid for tick bites —*
- Look for ticks and remove them.
- Remember you can become ill even after you have removed the tick and for as long as 8 days after you have left 'Tick country', so, if you feel ill, see a doctor and tell him you have been in 'Tick country'.

*Where the Honey bee is found*

# 15     The Honey bee

Australia has some native bees, but the most important bee from every point of view is the common or European Honey bee. These always seem busy; they spend most of their waking hours collecting nectar from flowers and bringing it back to the hive. If you disturb them, they can sting you with a very fine sting which is pushed out from the end of their bodies. The sting has little barbs on it and so, once it is pushed into your skin, the bee cannot remove it. When the bee flies away, it leaves the sting and poison gland behind. This hurts the bee so much that it soon dies.

44

The poison which is injected down the sting causes immediate sharp pain. If you don't get rid of the poison sac it will go on pumping poison down the sting and so the sting and poison sac should be removed as soon as possible by scraping them off with a finger nail. Do not try to pull the sting out as this will squeeze more venom down the sting and into the wound.

Some people become very sensitive to bee venom. After a sting they may get a rash over their bodies or become very short of breath. Sometimes they even die. Fortunately this allergy usually develops quite slowly and doctors can treat it before it gets too severe.

Never drink directly from a can of soft drink outside. Bees and wasps (see pages 46–7) can fly inside the can when you are not looking and, if you accidently swallow a bee or a wasp, it may sting the back of your throat and you may choke to death. *ALWAYS* use a straw or pour the can into a glass.

Bees love the clover growing on lawns and you may get stung if you play barefooted in summer. Ask your mum or dad to spray the lawn to get rid of clover.

*First aid for bee stings —*
• See pages 11 and 13.

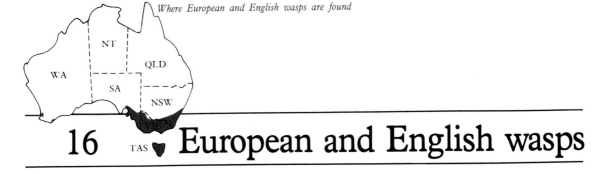

# 16 European and English wasps

(An English wasp. Photo: Vern Draffin)

Over the last few years, these wasps have been quietly spreading across the eastern parts of Australia and they are going to be an even bigger menace in the future. The map shows the area they had covered by April 1991. In Europe, many of the nests are destroyed by the cold winters. However, in most parts of Australia, they comfortably survive winter and get bigger and bigger each year. In Europe, the nests are often about the size of a football

46

and perhaps contain 6000 wasps. In Australia, some nests have been found more than 3 metres long and containing millions of wasps. The nests are usually at ground level and it is very dangerous to go near them, especially during the day. Most local councils will give you advice or arrange for the destruction of the nest.

The wasps are easy to spot because of their very bright yellow and dark brown colours. They do not appear to be frightened of anything, and will often zoom in on the family barbecue in a most unpleasant way. They like to get into soft drink cans (see pages 44–5).

They will just land on people's plates and proceed to take a piece of sausage or steak or drink up a little bit of tomato sauce. Try to shoo them away, and they will buzz up around your face and sometimes sting you. The sting is often more painful than a bee sting, and the wasp can sting a number of times. Its sting is not barbed like a bee sting and so it does not get stuck in the skin.

If wasps are about it is a good idea to spray the garden table and chairs before you start the outdoor lunch.

Sometimes wasp stings are very serious. Some people become very sensitive to wasp stings, like bee stings. When they are stung they must see a doctor at once.

**First aid for wasp stings —**
• See pages 11 and 13.

WASPS CAN REALLY GET UP YOUR NOSE!

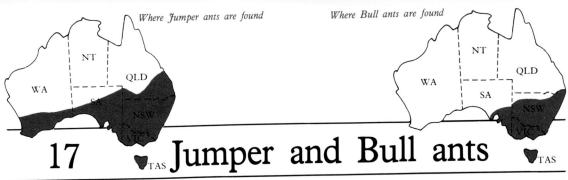

# 17  Jumper and Bull ants

(Jumper ant)

There are probably more than 20,000 of these pesky creatures in the bush for every human in Australia. Ever alert, they wait for the picnicker to arrive in the region of their nest. As you will see from the picture, they have a fine pair of nippers at the front end. These are used to grab hold of the victim. The ant then curls its body up and a long fine sting comes out of its behind and is driven into the target. The poison it injects burns and hurts you.

If undisturbed, the ant will usually sting a number of times. At a picnic, everyone soon knows that someone has been stung. They usually do a little bit of a dance, and often swear. If the ant has walked up inside someone's jeans, the victim disappears into the bush at high speed.

(Bull ant)

Unfortunately, many people have become very sensitive to ant poison, especially to Jumper ant poison. A single sting can make these people collapse and even kill them. Scientists at the Commonwealth Serum Laboratories are trying to find a safe treatment for them. In the meantime, they have to take great care to avoid contact with Jumper ants.

Ants like these are only found in Australia. They are a very old type of ant, and were busily using their venom to defend their nests millions of years before humans appeared on earth.

*First aid for ant stings —*
• See pages 11 and 13.

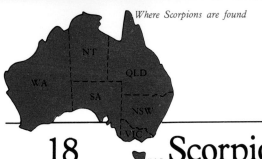

# 18 Scorpions

Australian scorpions are not as dangerous as those found in places like the Middle East and Mexico. You are not likely to get seriously ill after a sting by one of our scorpions. The further north you go, however, the bigger the scorpions are and the greater the amount of poison they can inject.

Scorpions grab their prey with their big front claws and then drive home their sting which is on the tip of their tails. In humans, the poison produces a very sharp pain which can last for some hours, but in the southern parts of Australia most scorpion stings are little worse than bee stings. It is pretty rare to be stung by a scorpion so people don't become sensitive to their poison as they do to ant and bee stings.

Scorpions are quite cute little creatures and in the bush can often be found resting under small rocks. So keep your eyes open and take care where you put your hands!

***First aid for Scorpion stings —***
* No first aid required.

# 19 The Platypus

(Close-up of spur)

Most people know that the platypus is a mammal which lays eggs. They know it has a front end which looks like a duck, and it is has a beautiful fur coat which keeps it nice and warm as it swims around hunting for yabbies and worms. What most people don't know is that the male platypus can give a sting which causes terrible pain.

Inside each rear leg of the male platypus is a poison spur and when he grips another platypus (or a fisherman's arm!) with his legs, the spur injects poison. Fishermen have cried because the sting hurts so much.

It is not certain why the platypus has this poison spur. It may be just to defend itself and its family, or it may have something to do with its mating habits.

*NEWS FLASH!* It has just been discovered that the platypus can find yabbies, etc., under water, in the dark, by detecting the tiny bits of electricity given off by these creatures. Little spots on the platypus's beak receive this information. Scientists have discovered that the platypus will find the tiniest battery, even when it is well hidden under rocks. I wonder what other secrets the platypus has kept from us?

*First aid for Platypus stings —*
• See page 13.

# 20 Blue-ringed octopus

Like the Red-back spider this little octopus has colours which warn you that it is dangerous. Normally it has dull yellow-brown bands with blue circles on its arms and body, but when it is disturbed its colours go dark and the rings become a bright peacock blue.

It has a tiny beak where its 8 arms join and, although it won't bite you in the water, it may if you pick it up. This octopus is the only very dangerous one in the world and carries enough poison to paralyse 10 adults. Usually it uses this poison to kill crabs so it can eat them without having to fight them first.

People have died after carrying this octopus on their arms. If you pick it up it will try to escape since it can't breathe when out of the water. It only bites when it is really upset and feels it is about to die. The victim doesn't usually feel the bite, but will very quickly become dizzy and paralysed.

If someone is bitten by this octopus the first aid is the same as for snake bite and the victim may also need help with breathing.

Never touch these little creatures. If you see them in a rock pool just poke them with a stick and watch the beautiful colour changes!

 *First aid for Blue-ringed octopus bites —*
- Pressure/immobilisation technique, see pages 9-10.
- Mouth to mouth resuscitation may be needed, see page 12.

WHEN ANGRY, THE BLUE-RINGED OCTOPUS SHOWS HIS TRUE COLOURS!

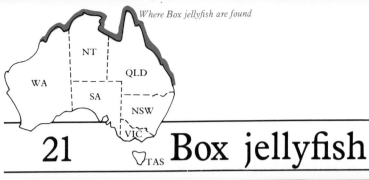

# 21  Box jellyfish

In 1956 a new tropical killer was discovered in Northern Queensland. Over the years about 60 swimmers had died within minutes of being stung by some animal, but it had never been found. Most stings happened on cloudy dull days when the sea was calm. A swimmer, usually a child, suddenly gave a terrible scream, stumbled out of the water and fell over. Victims looked as if they had been struck with whips because their bodies were covered with long red lines. The ones that didn't die had awful scars for the rest of their lives.

This tropical killer was the Box jellyfish. It is sometimes called the 'Sea wasp', but this is a bad name as some visitors have been known to keep looking up into the sky for it in case it is flying about! It is one of the few jellyfish which can kill a person and when fully grown it has a body the size of a laundry bucket. Ribbons of tentacles stream out from the body and are covered with millions and millions of stinging capsules. The Box jellyfish uses these to sting and kill fish. Then the tentacles pull the dead fish up to its mouth.

When a swimmer bumps into this jellyfish the thin tentacles get torn off, stick to the victim and inject their poison into the body. Victims should be taken out of the water and vinegar (never methylated spirits) poured over the jelly-like tentacles sticking to them. This kills the tentacles so they can be removed without injecting more poison. People who are badly stung may need help with their breathing and the doctor may give them antivenom.

The golden rule is never to swim in tropical waters if the local people say the Box jellyfish may be coming in near the shore. Usually 'Jellyfish warnings' are broadcast over radio stations and the lifesavers close the beaches. Don't swim by yourself in the tropics — people may never know what happened to you.

*First aid for Box jellyfish stings —*
- Pour vinegar (never methylated spirits) over tentacles on victim's body.
- Mouth to mouth resuscitation, see page 12, and antivenom may be needed.
- Seek medical care.

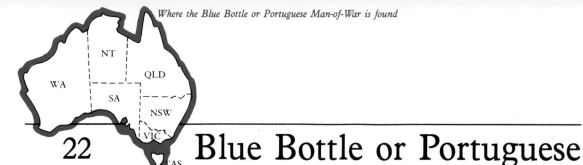

# 22 Blue Bottle or Portuguese Man-of-War

(Photo: Queensland Surf Rescue)

This is a common jellyfish which is found in the warmer seas of the world. The Blue Bottle is actually a number of jellyfish that have all joined together. Its top part has a lot of bubbles which make it light and help it catch the breeze so it sails across the water. Its stinging tentacles float underneath and these may be as long as 10 metres. The arrival of these jellyfish will close many beaches around the world.

Swimmers often come in contact with these jellyfish which can give quite painful stings, although they are nowhere as painful as those produced by the Box jellyfish (page 54). Severe stingings have sometimes killed people. The stings often have a ladder-like shape which mirrors the position of the stinging capsules on each tentacle.

Even bits of the jellyfish which have been broken off can float around and cause injuries sometime later. Swimmers' eyes are sometimes damaged by small pieces of jellyfish.

***First aid for Blue Bottle stings —***
• See page 13.

56

# 23 Stingrays

(Photo: Rudi H. Kuiter)

Stingrays can grow to be very big indeed. Some may reach 2 metres wide and over 4 metres in length. The actual tail is quite harmless, but at its base is a sting. Stingrays often lie on the bottom of the sea and if you stand on them, or swim near them, they give a sudden thrust of the tail which drives the sting into you.

Their tail works like a trigger, so the sting is driven in with terrible force. It has poison on it, and the wound is extremely painful and often bleeds a great deal. Two Australians have died when the sting actually entered their hearts.

Stingrays are very hard to see when they are resting on the seabed. It is best to go swimming with lots of other people and last in the water is probably safest.

***First aid for Stingray stings —***
• See page 13.

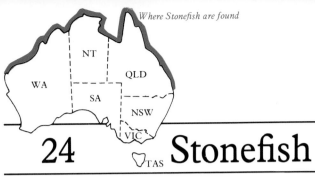

# 24 Stonefish

Stonefish are a very good reason for not walking about in tropical waters barefoot. Stand on a Stonefish and it's off to hospital for at least a week. They have 13 very sharp poisonous spines along their backs.

Stonefish are the most dangerous stinging fish in the world. When you tread on one the spines stick up straight and inject their poison deep into your foot. If you put your hand on one caught on a fishing line it's the end of your hand for a while. The poison makes your foot or hand terribly painful and swollen and can also affect the muscles of your body.

Even an expert can have trouble spotting a Stonefish as it sits in the shallow waters of coral reefs or mud flats. It may grow to a length of 47 cm, is covered with greenish slime and half buries itself in the sand. Its beady little eyes are watching for any passing fish which it will suddenly suck in by opening its giant mouth. Some people think it is like an older brother or sister or a politician — it sits around doing nothing all day, it has a big mouth and can prove highly venomous if you try to shift it!

Although Stonefish stings like other fish stings can be made less painful by bathing in warm water, usually pain killing drugs and antivenom from the doctor are needed. Remember, most stings occur during the school holidays — so take care.

 *First aid for Stonefish stings —*
- Bathe injured area in warm water.
- Seek medical care — antivenom may be needed.

BEWARE OF STONEFISH IF YOU PADDLE WITH SOFT LITTLE FEET!

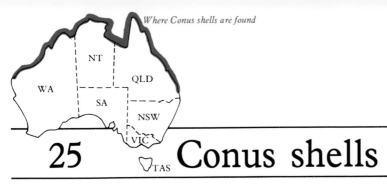
# 25 Conus shells

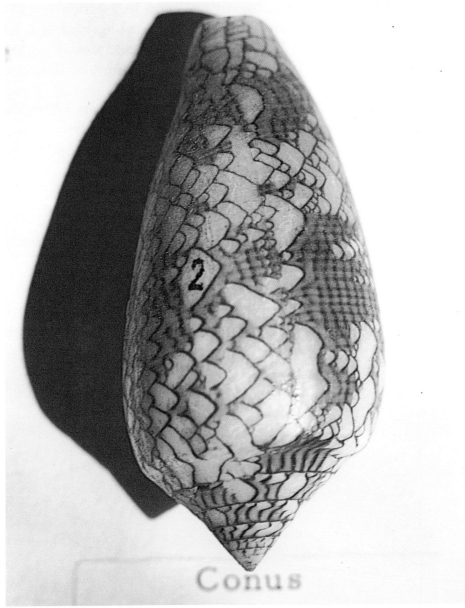

Conus

Conus shells are like sea-going garden snails, but they're not quite as harmless to humans. One type can kill a man!

The dangerous Conus shells live in tropical waters. They spend most of their time buried in sand, but move around at night to look for a new base if the hunting has not been good. They have a special way of catching their food. When a Conus shell sees a nice little fish coming by, it moves its mouth outwards and from there pushes a little poison dart into the fish. The fish is quickly killed by the poison and held close to the Conus shell by the dart. Its mouth then closes over the fish which is slowly swallowed. About 20 or 30 of these little darts are kept soaking in a pool of poison at the bottom of the shell's mouth. The darts are not used again and more are being made all the time.

Conus shells are often very beautiful and people love collecting them. However, if you pick one up with the owner still alive inside you could be in *dead* trouble!

A few years ago, a man held one in his hand on Hayman Island and it fired its little dart into him. He died some hours later from paralysis. Another person put one in his pocket and he got a nasty shock a few minutes later. Many people are stung when they are cleaning the shells as, like some of us, this creature does not like soap and scrubbing brushes.

The shells should not be picked up with bare hands even at the blunt end, as the animal can almost reach there with its dart. They should only be picked up with thick leather gloves or a pair of tongs.

If someone is stung the first aid is the same as for snake bite. The victim may need some help with breathing if the sting is bad.

*First aid for Conus shell stings —*
- Pressure/immobilisation technique, see pages 9-10.
- Mouth to mouth resuscitation may be needed, see page 12.

# 26 Toad and Puffer fish

These fish are very poisonous and should never be eaten. The very strong poison is found in the flesh of the fish as well as its insides. It is tasteless and not destroyed by heat and so cooking does not make these fish safe.

They are often caught off jetties and piers and come in all shapes and sizes. Most are only about 10 cm long. The biggest one ever caught was 76 cm in length. They have very big eyes and their sharp strong teeth are joined together to make four big teeth. No one seems to like them.

When pulled out of the water they usually puff themselves up with air and become like a ball. Some have spikes which stick out as they swell up. None of these fish have scales and so it is a good idea never to eat fish which have no scales. Even if you are starving these fish should not be eaten — the poison attacks the nerves and you may stop breathing.

If someone has eaten even a bit of one of these fish they should be made to vomit by tickling the back of their throat, if they are not unconscious, and then be taken to a doctor.

Incidentally, watch out for Toad and Puffer fish teeth! Sometimes they will nip off the end of a finger or a toe!

*First aid for Toad and Puffer fish poisoning —*
• Make the victim vomit.
• Seek medical care.
• Mouth to mouth resuscitation may be needed (see page 12).

# Other Poisonous Animals

Only the most poisonous Australian animals have been described in this book. Apart from the other kinds of poisonous snakes, there are many creatures which can and do make people ill.

On the land there are other kinds of spiders which give very painful bites.

In the sea, there are dozens of types of stinging fish and jellyfish which can all ruin a holiday.

There are some larger books which describe these land and sea creatures in detail. Look for them in your local library.

Remember, if you take a bit of care you should never be bitten or stung. When you know what the animals look like and keep a safe distance away neither the animal nor you will be harmed.

## FURTHER READING

You will find more information about Australia's poisonous animals and plants in —

*Venomous Creatures of Australia* published by Oxford University Press and *Family Guide to Dangerous Animals and Plants of Australia.*